Grandmother Time Anytime

Grandmother Time Anytime

Judy Gattis Smith

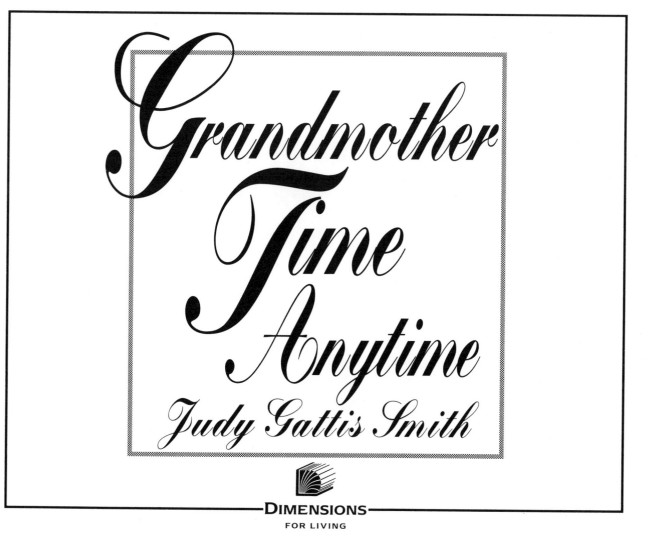

DIMENSIONS FOR LIVING

NASHVILLE

GRANDMOTHER TIME, ANYTIME

Copyright © 1994 by Dimensions for Living

94 95 96 97 98 99 00 01 02 03—10 9 8 7 6 5 4 3 2 1

Smith, Judy Gattis, 1933–
    Grandmother time, anytime / Judy Gattis Smith
       p.   cm.
    ISBN 0-687-02261-4 (pbk. : alk. paper)
    1. Christian education of children. 2. Grandparent and child. 3. Christian education—Home training.
4. Grandmothers—Religious life. 5. Bible games and puzzles. I. Title.
    BV1475.2.S634 1994
    248.8′45—dc20
                                                       93-38915
                                                          CIP

Scripture quotations are from the New Revised Standard Version Bible, Copyright 1989 by the Division of Christian Education of the National Council of the Churches of Christ in the USA. Used by Permission.

MANUFACTURED IN THE UNITED STATES OF AMERICA

For
Sarah-Neel Smith
Anna Rebecca Smith
Laura Rush Scott
Lisa Neel Scott

Contents

Introduction

Welcome to the Grandmother Club! If you have been gifted with God's wonderful present of a new second-generation life, you are a member. Our group includes a wide range of ages, of life-styles, of nationalities. We even include grandfathers. Our goal is to celebrate and enjoy and pass on our faith to these, our precious grandchildren. We are unabashed in our pride. We show pictures and tell grandchild stories at the slightest invitation. We are humble in our thanks and loud in our praise. We are grandmothers!

This is a book to use in your special time with your grandchild. It is a collection of many things: songs and stories and games. Be a user of this book, rather than a reader. You don't have to start at page 1 and read through to the end. Just flip through the book. Flip, read, and enjoy! My hope is that these ideas will encourage you to try out your own ideas; there is space for you to write those ideas. What games did you enjoy playing as a child? What was your childhood like? What traditions from your background would you like to pass on? And most important—how can we impart our Christian faith to a new generation?

In this age of high-tech, where everything flashes and whizzes and beeps, we focus on the simple things: walking hand-in-hand with our grandchild, singing and rocking, entering into the joy of playing together. But grandmother time is not a call back to the past, to the good old days, to a past time that was better. Grandmother time is a call to the present—a relating to the coming generation with all our past experience and knowledge as tools.

I have tried to pick up ideas and activities children have loved through the years—the movement and rhythms that seem to have a natural affinity with childhood—and then I have tried to recycle these ideas with biblical stories and Christian values that will support us in the coming years.

We have already received the blessing wished for in Psalm 128:6: "May you see your children's children." This book invites you to enhance and enjoy that blessing. ❧

Judy Gattis Smith

Grandmother Time Anytime

CHAPTER ONE

In Grandmother's Lap

♪ *Jesus loves me, this I know.* ♪

Dear Grandmother,

The very first memory I have of my maternal grandmother is of being rocked in a soft, ample lap as she sang, "Will there be any stars in my crown?"

Grandmother's lap is a special place—a place to soothe, a safe place for first play. Traditional lap songs and games have been enjoyed for years, handed down from generation to generation. We absorb these traditions as well as learn them in a logical way. I unconsciously find myself singing or humming "Will there be any stars in my crown?" as I rock my grandbabies, and I don't even know the song and can't recall having heard it for years.

In this chapter we pick up traditional lap favorites, some songs, some games, some fingerplays, and recycle them with Bible stories. Often just a snippet of the story is included, so the Bible reference where the whole story can be found is included. Why not begin to introduce children in this way, in their very earliest learnings, to our religious ancestors and traditions? Even without understanding the stories, children become familiar with the names.

Lap songs are not so much sung as crooned, so it doesn't matter whether you sing on key or with perfect tone. What's important is the joy and love your voice and nearness express.

Finding their fingers and being able to wiggle and control them is a great early adventure for babies. Sharing this adventure playfully and introducing names from our religious heritage can be a bonding experience. ❧

J.

1. FIVE MEN WHO FOLLOWED JESUS

(Mark 1:16-20; Luke 5:27)

Variation of the fingerplay "Where Is Thumbkin?"

1. First came Andrew.
First came Andrew
Here I am.
Here I am.
Go and follow Jesus.
Go and follow Jesus.
Yes I will.
Yes I will.

2. Then came Simon.
Then came Simon.
Here I am.
Here I am.
Go and follow Jesus.
Go and follow Jesus.
Yes I will.
Yes I will.

3. Where is James?
Where is James?
Here I am.
Here I am.
Go and follow Jesus.
Go and follow Jesus.
Yes I will.
Yes I will.

4. Where is John?.
Where is John?
Here I am.
Here I am.
Go and follow Jesus.
Go and follow Jesus.
Yes I will.
Yes I will.

5. Come on Levi.
   Come on Levi.
   Here I am.
   Here I am.
   Go and follow Jesus.
   Go and follow Jesus.
   Yes I will.
   Yes I will.

Grandmother, holding the baby in her lap, chants the words and does the following motions. Baby imitates.

On verse 1, first one thumb is held up, then the other.
On "Here I am" the thumbs wiggle at each other.
On "Come and follow Jesus" the thumbs continue to wiggle.
On "Yes I will" first one hand, then the other, disappears behind the back.
Successive fingers follow the same pattern.
Create a new verse using baby's name.

2. JESUS' MIRACLE AT CANA

(John 2:1-11)

variation of "I'm a Little Teapot"

I'm an empty wine jar,
   short and stout.
Here is my handle.
Here is my spout.
Jesus filled me up
   and now I shout.
Just tip me over and
   pour me out.

Grandmother places one hand on her hip for the handle, extending the other arm, bent at the wrist and elbow for the spout. The child copies the action. On "tip me over," Grandmother and child bend over at the waist toward the extended arm as if pouring out of the jar.

3. THE BOY WITH THE LOAVES AND FISHES

(Luke 9:12-17)

A variation of that old favorite finger game, "Here's the Church"

Two little fishes (*hold up two fingers of one hand*).
Five loaves of bread (*hold up the other hand with all fingers open*).
He gave these to Jesus (*lock the fingers, knuckle to knuckle*).
And everyone was fed (*invert so that the fingers are pointing upward; wiggle the fingers*).

4. JOSHUA AT JERICHO

(Joshua 6:1-21)

fingerplay

One, two, three, four, five, six, seven days
They marched around the town.
The trumpet blew. The wall fell down.
One, two, three, four, five, six, seven.

Baby sits in Grandmother's lap, facing Grandmother. Using Grandmother's fingers like a pair of legs, walk up the child's arm. At the "wall fell down," tilt the child slightly backward, holding securely. Then on the final counting let the fingers run back down the arm.

5. PALM SUNDAY PARADE

(Mark 11:1-11)

Variation of "The Wheels on the Bus Go Round and Round"

This is the way that Jesus rode
Up and down, up and down.
This is the way that Jesus rode
Into Jerusalem town.
(bounce child on your knee)

The children shouted,
"Hosannah! Hosannah! Hosannah!"
The children shouted
"Hosannah!"
Into Jerusalem town.
(wave arms back and forth as if waving palm branches)

The Pharisees said,
"We'll get you! We'll get you! We'll get you!"
The Pharisees said,
"We'll get you!"
Into Jerusalem town.
(shake fists)

Jesus kept riding
Right on through. Right on through. Right on through.
Jesus kept riding
Right on through.
Into Jerusalem town.
(bounce on knees again)

6. JOSEPH'S BROTHERS

(Genesis 37:22)

a tuneless game

Here come Joseph's brothers,
Big, strong men.

Watch out for the pit.
You're going to fall in!

Grandmother holds child on knees facing her. Hold both hands. Bounce the child up and down in rhythm to the words. On the last line, Grandmother opens legs and the child falls in. Keep holding tight to the hands!

Do you remember these old favorite lap games? While baby is still in your lap, you might want to play them: Patty-Cake, Peek-a-boo, Eeensy-Weensy Spider, and This Little Piggie Went to Market. The rhythm, the touching, the fun together are the important things.

Each culture has some of these lap songs. Reach back in the recesses of your memory for other lap songs and games you remember that may have been stored there since your childhood.

Or create new ones. These first simple games can be gentle ways of learning. Walk your fingers up the baby's chest, over his face, and down his back. The baby will chortle and so will you. My granddaughters loved the very simple little game where I, with two fingers, would very gently close their eyelids and chant "Shut, little eyes." As soon as my fingers were removed, their eyes would pop open and they would laugh and laugh. Unless they were very sleepy!

A grandmother I know rocks her grandchild to sleep in her lap with a "loveaby" rather than a lullaby.

Write a lap song or chant you remember here:

CHAPTER TWO

In Grandmother's Kitchen

♪ *Let us break bread together on our knees.* ♪

Dear Grandmother,

Our faith and our food are the two things most closely linked to our daily lives. In our families our moments of greatest joy and deepest sorrow usually include food.

Grandmother's kitchen today may be anything

—from the traditional storybook image of a flour-dusted granny baking cookies and biscuits over a huge stove
—to the high-tech kitchen of a career granny in an efficiency condo
—to the cubby hole section of a retirement apartment or room.

Our setting need not determine our ability to enjoy creating and sharing food with our grandchildren.

The first ideas in this section seek to combine the memorization of a Scripture passage with the creation of a salad by Grandmother and grandchild working together. In most of these recipes the ingredients are only suggestions. Most ideas are more for arranging the food to suggest the Bible verse, rather than the cooking of it. Feel free to substitute other ingredients. The more creative the better!

This time of working together offers unique possibilities for that one-on-one conversation with your grandchild. Questions are suggested to begin the conversation flow. Encourage the child to say more by responding "I see"; "Okay"; "Tell me more"; "Really?"; "Hmmm."

J.

SCRIPTURE SALADS

1. Verse to memorize: Psalm 119:105—"Your word is a lamp to my feet and a light to my path."

Candle Salad

Place a slice of pineapple on each salad plate. Place half of a peeled banana upright inside the pineapple. Add a dab of mayonnaise to the top of the banana and top it off with a maraschino cherry.

Talk it over: This is a good Advent salad, as we await the coming of Christ, the Light of the world. Discuss the meaning of Advent with your grandchild. Ask: "Do you remember a time you were in the dark and someone brought a light? Tell me about it."

2. Verse to memorize: Psalm 104:24—"O LORD, how manifold are your works! In wisdom you have made them all; the earth is full of your creatures."

Creature Salad

mandarin oranges
chopped peanuts
lettuce
animal crackers

Toss oranges and peanuts. Spoon onto lettuce-lined bowl. Place animal crackers on top and marching around the edge.

Talk it over: Talk to your grandchildren about all the wonderful creatures that God has created to share the world with us. Explain that *manifold* means "many." How many creatures can the children name? What is their favorite animal? If they could be an animal, what would they be?

3. Verse to memorize: Psalm 128:1-2—"Happy is everyone who fears the LORD, who walks in his ways. You shall eat the fruit of the labor of your hands; you shall be happy, and it shall go well with you."

Happy Face Salad

Place one chilled peach half on a bed of cottage cheese. Create a happy face with raisin eyes, cherry nose, and apple slices for mouth and ears.

Talk it over: Explain to your grandchild that "fearing" the Lord does not mean being afraid of God but greatly respecting God. Ask: "What's funny about yourself that makes you smile when you think of it? Tell me three things that make you happy."

4. Verse to memorize: Psalm 133:1—"How very good and pleasant it is when kindred live together in unity!"

Family Ring Mold

2 packages lemon-flavored gelatin
1½ cups hot water
2 cups fruit syrup (drained from peaches and pineapples)
peach halves, drained
pineapple slices, drained
dark sweet cherries

Prepare gelatin with hot water and syrup. In an 8-inch ring mold place pineapple slices with a cherry in the center. Stand peach halves upright. Carefully pour the gelatin over the fruit; chill until firm. Caution! It's hot!

Talk it over: Ask your grandchild: "Do you know what the word *kindred* means? Unity?" Why is a circular salad a good symbol for a family? Ask: "What would you change about our family if you had the power? What worries you about our family?"

5. Verse to memorize: Psalm 67:1—"May God be gracious to us and bless us and make his face to shine upon us."

Sunshine Salad

2 3-ounce packages orange-flavored gelatin
1 pint orange sherbet
1 11-ounce can mandarin oranges (drained)
   Dissolve gelatin in two cups boiling water. Add sherbet and blend well. Fold in oranges. Pour into a round mold and chill until set.

Talk it over: Ask: "What are some ways God has already blessed us? What is the best thing that could ever happen to you?"

6. Verse to memorize: Psalm 71:17-18—"O God, from my youth you have taught me, and I still proclaim your wondrous deeds. So even to old age and gray hairs, O God, do not forsake me, until I proclaim your might to all the generations to come."

Old Man Salad

Stuff pitted, cooked prunes with cream cheese.

Talk it over: Ask: "What do you think growing old is like? What do you think is good about it? What is bad about it? How old is old?"

7. Verse to memorize: Psalm 121:1—"I lift up my eyes to the hills—from where will my help come? My help comes from the LORD, who made heaven and earth."

Mountain Salad

Put canned pear halves together with cream cheese. Stand upright. Top with watercress.

Talk it over: Ask: "What mountain or hill have you seen? If you were a mountain, what would it feel like? If you climbed to the top of a mountain, what would you see?"

8. Verse to memorize: Psalm 17:8—"Guard me as the apple of the eye."

Cinnamon Apples

2 cups sugar
1 cup water
⅓ cup cinnamon candy or sticks of cinnamon
red food coloring
Pare and core apples. Cook in syrup until tender.

Talk it over: "Apple of the eye" is a funny expression. Ask your grandchild what he or she thinks it means. Ask: "In all of our language, what is the most beautiful word you know?"

9. Verse to memorize: Isaiah 49:1b—"The LORD called me before I was born, while I was in my mother's womb he named me."

> **"Me" Veggie Salad**
>
> body: flat wedge of lettuce or leaf lettuce to make a dress
> arms and legs: small celery or carrot sticks
> head: half of a hard-boiled egg
> eyes and nose: olive bits
> mouth: pimento strip
> hair: grated yellow cheese
>
> *Talk it over:* Ask: "Is anyone in the world *exactly* like you? What is special about you?"

A STIR-UP OUR HEARTS PUDDING

"Stir up, we beseech thee, O Lord, the wills of thy faithful people."

In England, years ago, this scripture passage gave rise to a day called "Stir-up Sunday." On this day the housewives began to make (and stir up) their Christmas puddings.

Using this idea, create with your grandchild a pudding from a family recipe or an instant pudding mix. After filling pudding cups, let your grandchild bury a candy cinnamon heart in one. There may be only one pudding serving with a special heart to be discovered while eating, or, as is more likely if your grandchild is helping, all puddings will have a hidden heart. *Talk it over:* Talk about surprises. What other ways can you create special surprises for others?

THE MICROWAVE AND MOSES

Use the microwave to tell a Bible story? Why not?

Place a bag of microwave popcorn in your microwave oven and follow package directions for popping. As you are waiting, tell your grandchildren this story:

Remember our ancestor Moses and how he led the people of Israel out of slavery in Egypt? Moses went to the great pharaoh and pleaded with him to let the Hebrew people go free. And when the pharaoh refused, God sent plagues on the land. There were mighty signs and miracles until the pharaoh gave up and said, "Go!" Then all the Hebrew people, six hundred thousand men with their wives, marched out of Egypt. The children went too, of course, early in the morning without even waiting to eat breakfast.

God continued to show great power and miracles. When the people came to the Red Sea, it parted for them to cross. Great walls of water were on either side, but the people marched through. The children went too, leaving small footprints on the sea floor.

After this, they crossed the great Wilderness of Shur. God guided them every day with a cloud that moved in front of them. At night, when they rested, God watched over them through a pillar of fire. And little children looked up at the cloud as they walked and walked, taking many little steps to keep up with the adults. They knew God was going with them. At night, the last thing the children saw before closing their eyes was a pillar of fire, and they knew God was watching over them by night.

Finally they all arrived at a place called the Wilderness of Sin. The children were tired of traveling and became fretful, and so did the adults. They could not find food enough to feed them, and you know how fussy and fretful people become when they are hungry. They forgot how they had suffered in Egypt. They forgot that God always led them and took care of them. And the adults complained, and some of the children cried. They wanted to go back, and they thought they were going to die.

But God said to Moses, "I did not bring the people all this way to die." God had a wonderful plan. While the people were sleeping that night it began to happen.

(By now the corn should be popping. Tell the children to shut their eyes and listen and smell.)

God was sending a wonderful food. It was small, like a wafer, and white. In the morning it covered all the ground around them. When the people saw it they asked, "What is it?" And the children ran and looked at it and smelled it and tasted it and said, "What is it?" In their language the words "What is it?" are *man hu,* and so the food afterward came to be called "manna."

(By now the popcorn should be ready)

We don't have to ask what this food is. We know it is popcorn. But the same God who provided good things for the children of Israel provides good things for us today. Eat and enjoy and remember—our God looks after us.

Popping corn produces joy for all our senses. We listen to the pop. We see it move and change shape. We smell its tantalizing aroma. We touch its bumpy texture. We eat it up!

MICROWAVE DANIEL'S PLATE

Daniel's Vegetables

1 small head cauliflower
1 bunch broccoli florets
3 or 4 carrots, sliced ¼ inch
½ cup melted butter
½ tsp. garlic salt
¼ tsp. pepper
    With your help, let your grandchild create this dish. Place cauliflower in the center of a round microwave dish. Arrange broccoli and carrots around the outside. Melt butter and pour over the vegetables. Sprinkle with garlic salt and pepper. Cover with plastic wrap, turning one edge up. Microwave on high 17-19 mins.

As the platter is cooking, read Daniel 1 from your Bible. Because of the unusual names in this story, it is best read by you or an older child. This may lead to a discussion of nutrition, of what foods your grandchild likes and dislikes and why.

FED BY RAVENS

I Kings 17:1-6

When neighbors unexpectedly bring in food, we sometimes say, "We are being fed by ravens." We say this because of a Bible story, and here is the story:

It had not rained for many days. The grass was brown and the flowers dead. The ground was hard and cracked.

A man named Elijah was a prophet of God. God spoke to him and said, "Go and live by the brook named Cherith, and you will have water to drink."

The place was far away from other people, and Elijah wondered if he would die there from hunger. But he always did what God told him to do.

The morning after he arrived, he looked up and saw some large black birds circling overhead. They had pieces of bread (or something) in their mouths. Elijah stood very still and quiet and waited.

The birds landed close to Elijah. He could see the shiny gloss of their black wings. Strutting toward him, staring hard with unblinking bird eyes, they approached so close he could have reached out and touched them. Then they opened their beaks, dropped the bread and meat they were carrying in front of him, and with a loud croaking cry and whir of wings rose swiftly into the sky and were gone.

Elijah stared in disbelief at the food that had appeared from nowhere. He ate gratefully and thanked God.

In the evening as the sun was setting, there, over the horizon, appeared the birds again.

Day after day, morning and night, Elijah was fed by the ravens. God was taking care of Elijah, just as God had promised.

Fed-by-the-Ravens-Peanut Butter Balls

½ cup crunchy peanut butter
¾ cup nonfat dry milk
½ cup honey
1 cup wheat germ
   Combine all ingredients. Mix well and shape into walnut-sized balls. Roll in additional wheat germ. Fly around to members of your family and drop a cookie in their mouths—like ravens feeding Elijah.

It's a lovely tradition to serve your grandchild's favorite dish when she visits. And when you cook and serve your grandchild's very favorite food, remember Psalm 34:8—"O taste and see that the LORD is good."

DYED EASTER ONIONS

For something different this Easter, try dying onions instead of eggs. It's a fun experience to share with your grandchild. You will need to collect these things:

small sprouting onions
empty vegetable cans
pieces of crayons (lots)
electric fry pan
stick to stir with

1. Peel the dry skin from the onions.
2. Place the crayon pieces in the vegetable cans, a different color in each can. Use enough crayon pieces to cover the onions once the crayons are melted.
3. Place the cans with the crayons in the electric fry pan. Fill the pan with water to about ¼ the height of the cans.
4. Bring the water to simmer.
5. Stir the crayons until they melt.
6. Holding an onion by its sprouts, or using a long-handled fork, dip it into the melted wax.
7. Place the onion on a paper towel until the wax hardens. You'll love the colors!
8. Arrange the onions in a basket. They will continue to sprout, and you can cut off the tips and use them in salads.

A regular sauce pan on the stove may be used instead of the electric fry pan.

KITCHEN PLAY

Don't forget that your kitchen can be a wonderful playground for grandchildren. Is there a toddler anywhere who doesn't like to explore the pots and pans drawer? There they are—clanging lids together like cymbals, drumming on pans with a wooden spoon, putting little pans inside bigger pans, putting a sauce pan on his or her head for a helmet, trying to sit in a frying pan. Their curiosity and creativity never cease to amaze.

The canned food shelf offers opportunities for stacking and building, arranging and exploring. Cookie cutters can be lined up in a parade. Unbreakable mixing bowls offer unique possibilities. Measuring spoons and spatulas are personified. Who needs store-bought toys when there are opportunities to use hands-on, real cooking objects and the imagination?

AROMA PICTURE

How many of us associate Grandmother's kitchen with smells—wonderful aromas of baking bread or spicy apple pies or the deep rich aroma of coffee or chocolate? Nothing is more memorable than a smell.

As your grandchild explores your kitchen, open your spice rack for a sense-of-smell adventure.

Dilute white glue to a smooth watery consistency. Brush the glue on a plain sheet of paper and then allow your grandchild to shake a spice of choice onto the glue. Possibilities are paprika, black pepper, apple or pumpkin pie spice, curry powder, cloves, nutmeg, cinnamon. Use your imagination.

Carefully shake off the excess. Let dry. You have an aroma picture. Perhaps your grandchild would like to draw a picture that the smell suggests.

Draw a floor plan of the kitchen you remember from your childhood.

My kitchen at home—long ago

CHAPTER THREE

Grandmother's Stories

♪ *Tell me the story of Jesus, write on my heart every word.* ♪

Dear Grandmother,

    Throughout history grandmothers have passed on traditions and values through the stories we have told and retold. The image of a storyteller and a rapt audience is deep in our preconsciousness.
    In this section we will look at some old stories in a new way.

JELLY BEAN STORIES

Colors constantly affect us, whether we are aware of it or not. Imagine how dull life would be with the unrelieved monotony of no color. Some colors excite us; some soothe us. Some people associate certain colors with smelling good, such as pink, lavender, yellow, and green. Some people associate colors with music: oboe note of violet, cool woodwind of green, mellow piping of yellow, the bugle call of red, the sounding brass of orange. Children seem especially sensitive to color.

The following Bible stories are identified by colors. Because children tend to learn more quickly when they experience what they are trying to learn, they will be eating the colors in the form of jelly beans as they listen.

Choose jelly beans of the right color and urge the children to taste each jelly bean carefully as it slides down their throats. Tell them to imagine their bodies becoming that color.

A Red Jelly Bean Story

Red is the most dominant and dynamic color. It is an exciting color. We think of fire and blood and Valentines and Christmas and lobsters. Red directs us outward.

The story of Pentecost is a good red jelly bean story. You can find it in Acts 1:15–2:47.

As your grandchildren are eating red jelly beans, say:

Shut your eyes and try to imagine going up a set of stairs to a large room. When you enter the room you see many people—over a hundred. They are all quiet and waiting. But you feel energy and electricity in the room. These people are disciples and friends who had been with Jesus while he lived on earth. Jesus died. He was crucified. But some of these same people saw him on Easter morning and other times after he was raised. Jesus told them to wait for something special that was coming—here in this very room. You can feel the waiting and the excitement. What is coming? Remember how excited you feel when you wait for something—a surprise—to come?

The people are happy. What will it be?

Suddenly there is a sound like a rushing, mighty wind. Try to remember the sound of a powerful wind you have heard. It was spinning all around them.

Now imagine the people looking at each other and seeing the strangest thing. On everyone's head there seemed to be a tongue-shaped flame of fire. But it did not burn them at all. It just danced there.

With your eyes still closed, try to see the color red as vividly as you can on the screen of your closed eyelids. Can you see dancing flames?

As soon as the wind and the fire came, the people began to feel differently. They felt very powerful and very bold. And now the quiet room was quite noisy. People were shouting and laughing and jumping up and down. It was so noisy in fact that people outside heard them and stopped to look and listen. When the disciples saw the people gathering outside, the disciples ran down the steps and began to tell them all about Jesus and the wonderful gift that God had given them—a gift of power and joy that we call the Holy Spirit.

If you have a red sheet, blanket, or bedspread let your grandchild roll in red. Have the child lie face down and roll back and forth, the color surrounding him or her.

An Orange Jelly Bean Story

Orange is a pleasing color to most people. Studies say it has high appetite appeal. We think of pumpkins, oranges, and sweet potatoes. It is a warm, comfortable color.

Jesus' experience with the boy who shared his lunch is a good orange jelly bean story. You can find the story in Matthew 14:13-23; Mark 6:31-46; Luke 9:10-17; and John 6:1-15.

As your grandchildren are eating orange jelly beans, say:

Shut your eyes and try to imagine that you are a part of a large crowd of people who have been following Jesus all day. Jesus has been talking and healing people. So anxious are the people to hear Jesus and to have their loved ones healed that they press constantly upon him and allow no time for him to rest or even eat. They have been so interested that they have lost track of what time it is and how far they have come. It has been a long day, and few of the people brought anything to eat. Imagine how you would feel if you had missed a meal because you were far from home and, of course, there was no grocery store you could run to.

One boy in the crowd had not forgotten his lunch basket, and in his basket he carried five little loaves of barley bread and two small fishes.

Jesus became concerned for all the hungry people. He and the disciples began discussing what they could do to feed them. The boy who had not forgotten to bring his lunch came near and heard their conversation. What would you have done? Would you have run off behind a rock and gobbled up your lunch?

The boy handed his lunch to Jesus. I'm sure the boy was just as hungry as all the others. At first one of the disciples said, "This won't do any good. What will five little loaves mean to so many people? Just keep it, boy."

But Jesus had a better idea. He had all the people sit down. He took the little loaves and the fishes, and he began to pass the food among the hungry people.

Well, a miraculous thing happened! The baskets of food were shared, people ate, but the food did not give out. The people kept eating until all were satisfied, and there was still food left in the baskets. How could this be?

With your eyes still shut, try to picture baskets full of food. Think how good it must have tasted.

A Green Jelly Bean Story

The color green brings thoughts of cedar and wintergreen and growing things. It is a color that reduces nervousness and muscular tension. Studies show it is a good color for concentration. Imagine emeralds and new grass and olives and limes and fresh unfurling ferns.

The story of Zacchaeus is a good green jelly bean story. You can find it in Luke 19:1-10.

As your grandchildren are eating green jelly beans, say:

Shut your eyes and try to imagine you are living in an oasis called Jericho. Surrounding you are sandy deserts on all sides. But the town of Jericho is filled with shades of green—light green, dark green, leaf green, apple green, sea green, bottle green, pea green, emerald green—everything green-green.

One day Jesus came to this town. Everyone rushed out to see him. Among the crowd was a rich man named Zacchaeus. He had money and power, but he was short—very short. The people lining the road to see Jesus would not allow Zacchaeus to push in front of them. Have you ever gone to a parade and not been able to see because of the people in front of you? Maybe your father lifted you up to see—but Zacchaeus couldn't do that.

Zacchaeus had an idea. In this green-green town were green-green trees. With your eyes still shut, try to see green on the screen of your closed eyelids.

Not only could Zacchaeus see Jesus, but Jesus could see Zacchaeus, and when Jesus got directly under the tree he said, "Zacchaeus, come down at once, for I am coming to your house."

Can you imagine how fast Zacchaeus must have shimmied down that tree?

Zacchaeus was so happy he decided to share his wealth with the poor and never to take money unfairly from other people.

Jesus knew this little man had longed to see him, that Zacchaeus received him gladly in his home and had willingly tried to make his wrongs right.

Zacchaeus grew in goodness just like the tree grew leaves.

A Blue (or Lavender) Jelly Bean Story

You may have to go to a special store to find a blue jelly bean. Blue is a color that relaxes us. It soothes us. It lulls us. It is a good color for day dreaming. We think of blue skies or ocean waves or blue birds. Blue is like cool breezes.

If you cannot find a blue jelly bean, a lavender one will work with this story of Jacob's dream. You can find the story in Genesis 28.

As your grandchildren are eating blue (or lavender) jelly beans, say:

Shut your eyes and try to imagine you are running away from home—not because you want to, but because you have done something very wrong to your brother. This is what happened to Jacob, who lived in Bible times. Jacob had tricked his brother twice; once out of his father's blessing, and once out of his inheritance. His brother, whose name was Esau, was so mad he said he would kill Jacob. This was the reason Jacob was running. Can you imagine how lonely and frightened he must have been? And he probably felt very sorry, too. He had told his mother and his blind, elderly father "good-bye" and started on a long, lonely journey. He had no camel to ride on or anyone with him to talk to, and he didn't know if he would ever see his home again.

It must have been worse just as the sun was going down. Imagine poor Jacob all alone under a vast blue sky, defenseless and frightened. Was Esau following him to kill him? Would he ever see his mother again?

The path Jacob was traveling was rocky, and he lay down with a stone for a pillow.

While he slept he began to dream. The dream started with a blue sky—peaceful, serene, surrounding him. Then he saw a ladder reaching from earth up into this blue-blue sky. As he continued to dream he saw beautiful angels climbing up and down the ladder. At the top he saw God, and God spoke to him: "I am with you and will be with you wherever you go, and I will protect you and bring you again to this land. I will never leave you."

Jacob awoke from the dream and looked all around. Although he was still alone, he now knew God was with him. The journey ahead was still long and hard, but he was no longer afraid.

More Color Ideas

To add still another dimension to your color stories, try adding a musical tone. On the piano use the note, chord, or scale of:

C   for your red story

D   for your orange story

F   for your green story

B   for your blue story

Another color idea to go with your stories is to get a large stack of colored construction paper. Cut shapes and move them around to illustrate the color story.

Use the same color in different shades. Put a color of medium value between one of lighter on one side and darker value on the other. The middle color will look darker next to the light color and lighter on the edge next to the dark piece.

To make a color seem brighter put it against a gray background. To make it lighter put it against a dark background. Encourage your grandchildren to experiment.

VALUE STORIES—AESOP AND BODY MOVEMENT

Have you ever thought of your role as grandmother as that of value teacher? Though the primary teaching of values will come from parents, we can be a positive force for teaching values. If we and parents decline the challenge, children will learn their major values from peers or television, videos, and movies or more aggressive people.

At the same time that we want to be value teachers, we don't want to come across as nagging, sermonizing, or moralizing. Can the teaching of values be fun? To help us, we look at two ancient teaching methods.

For thousands of years, people have been enjoying the wise and funny fables of Aesop. These little stories look at the way people behave. They present human actions usually portrayed by animals.

For the second ancient method we look to India where thousands of years ago people watched the movements of insects, animals, and birds and devised body exercises to imitate these movements. We seek to combine these two methods: teaching wisdom through body movements.

Choose a place, preferably carpeted, where the child can move and stretch unhampered. Remove shoes. Wear comfortable clothes. Tell the Aesop fable, then help the child create the body movements. Encourage the child to learn in a new way—by listening to his or her body. The flexible body of a young child can move easily and gracefully into these positions. And while we are learning we are having fun.

The Monkey and the Camel

AESOP'S FABLE

Once upon a time there was a gathering of animals. A monkey danced with such skill that all the other animals applauded. A camel who was watching was jealous. He tried to dance in the same way, but only made a fool of himself, and all the animals laughed and made fun of him.

> **Moral:** *It's foolish to try to be what you aren't. A camel can't act like a monkey.*

Body Movement: Be a camel. Say to the child: "Kneel with your legs apart, hands on your waist. Then bend back. Grab hold of your ankles with your hands. Let your head hang back." You are a camel. *Think about the story.*

The Frog and the Rabbit

AESOP'S FABLE
AND BODY MOVEMENT

Once there was a rabbit. *(Invite your grandchild to sit on the floor, sitting on her heels. Say: "Hold on to your heels and bend forward slowly. Place the top of your head on the floor in front of you, close to your knees. You are now a rabbit, resting with your ears folded back.")*

Well, this rabbit was scared of everything. As soon as a single animal approached, off he would run. Or he would freeze in place and not move a muscle. *(Hold your position perfectly still without moving.)*

One day a troop of wild horses ran by the rabbit, and he was so scared he ran to a nearby lake ready to jump in and drown. He was so panicked. But a funny thing happened when he neared the lake. He saw a frog.

(Instruct the child to come out of the rabbit position by slowly sitting up until her back and head are in a straight line. Now invite your grandchild to become a frog. Say: "Still sitting on your heels, spread your knees far apart and try to touch your toes in back. Now sit firmly on the floor and not on your heels. You are a frog.")

The frog was greatly frightened by the rabbit, so he scuttled off and jumped into the water.

"Well," said the rabbit. "There is always someone worse off than yourself!"

(Come out of the frog position by bringing the knees together again and sitting on your heels. Think about the story.)

Belling the Cat

AESOP'S FABLE

The mice were greatly bothered by their old enemy, the cat. What could they do to protect themselves? Finally a young mouse said, "I know! Our problem is—the cat slips up on us before we know it. Now if we could receive some signal of her approach we could run to safety. I propose, therefore, that we get a bell and tie it around the cat's neck with a ribbon. Then we'll always hear the cat coming."

This proposal was met with great applause until an old mouse said, "But who will volunteer to put the bell around the cat's neck?" None of the mice volunteered.

Moral: *It's easy to suggest impossible things.*

Body Movement: Be a cat. Instruct the child to begin in a kneeling position. Say: "Spread your knees apart. Bend over and place your hands on the floor. You are now on all fours—like a cat. Slowly arch your back like an angry cat. Pull in your stomach and let your head hang down. Return to all fours, sink in your back and look away up. You are stretching one way, then the other, slowly, like a cat.

Think about the story.

The Ant and the Grasshopper

AESOP'S FABLE

One summer day an ant and a grasshopper met in the field. The grasshopper was chirping and singing and hopping about. The ant was working very hard carrying an ear of corn to his nest.

"Come and play," said the grasshopper.

"I have to lay up food for the winter," said the ant. "You'd better too."

"Phooey on winter" said the grasshopper, and he kept playing. The ant kept working.

When winter came the grasshopper had no food, but the ant had a good supply.

Moral: *It is best to be prepared.*

Body Movement: Be a grasshopper. Say to your grandchild: "Lie on your stomach with your arms at your sides, legs together, chin on the floor. Hold your arms close to your body and make fists with your hands, thumbs touching the floor. Now, all at the same time—take a deep breath, push down on the floor with your fists, and raise both legs together. As you breathe out, slowly lower both legs together."

Think about the story.

The Tortoise and the Hare

AESOP'S FABLE

Once a speedy hare was making fun of a slow-moving tortoise. To all the animals' surprise the tortoise challenged the hare to a race. The hare accepted, sped off, and was soon so far ahead the tortoise was nowhere to be seen. The hare decided to take a nap. As he was sleeping, the tortoise plodded by. He just kept on and kept on going in his slow, steady way. After a good nap the hare sped to the finish line—sure that he had won the race. What a surprise when he got there and found the tortoise already there.

Moral: *Slow and steady wins the race.*

Body Movement: Be a tortoise. (This may be difficult for tight muscled children.) Say to your grandchild: "Sit on the floor and spread your legs straight and wide apart. Put your arms under your legs with the palms down. Bend forward until your head touches the ground. You are a tortoise."

Think about the story.

BIBLE VERSES AND BODY POSITIONS

Isaiah 40:31—*"Those who wait for the* LORD *shall renew their strength, they shall mount up with wings like eagles."*

Movements

Balance on your tiptoes. Bend over and stretch your hands straight behind you—like wings. Feel the stretch and the balance. You are an eagle, ready to take off.

Psalm 1:3—*"They are like trees planted by streams of water, which yield their fruit in its season, and their leaves do not wither. In all they do, they prosper."*

Movements

Balance on your left leg, this is the tree trunk. Bend your right leg and place it, resting high, on your left leg; this is a twisted tree branch. Raise both arms overhead, fingertips touching; these are the leafy tips of the tree tops.

FAVORITE STORIES

The favorite stories are your "grandchild's story." Tell the child about her or his birth. What the day was like—the weather, the setting, the time when this unique child appeared in the world. Bringing out the photo albums may help trigger the memories. Tell stories about your

grandchildren that are *all* about them. Tell the children about ways they have been helpful to others. Reinforce with these stories their good feelings about themselves. Tell them about ways God has acted in their lives. Plant and cultivate the fact that each life has meaning and purpose. Tell them often what you like about them and the strengths you see in them.
Ephesians 2:10—"For we are what [God] has made us, created in Christ Jesus for good works, which God prepared beforehand to be our way of life."

Tell and retell these stories. Recognize the power of repetition. Children are deeply reassured by repetition. It suggests to them continuity and connection in a modern world that is often full of upheaval and disconnection.

The Legend of the Search for the Most Important

Once upon a time a young man set out on a journey to find three things:

1. the most important person in the world
2. the most important place in the world
3. the most important thing in the world

He met kings and queens. He met millionaires and billionaires. He met rock stars and famous generals. He met artists and musicians and scientists and presidents. But alas, none of these was the "most important person."

The young man traveled everywhere. He went with an astronaut to the moon. He went to the tallest building in the world. He sailed on the deepest, widest ocean. He went into a marble palace. Alas, none of these was the "most important place."

He tried everything. He learned to work the world's smartest computer. He took part in the Olympics and played in the Super Bowl. He drove the fastest car in the world. He read all the famous books in the world. Alas, none of these was the "most important thing."

He asked everyone he met, "Who is the most important person in the world? Where is the most important place? What is the most important thing to do?" He tried all their suggestions, but they did not satisfy him. He became discouraged and sad.

Then one day, sitting alone under a tree in his yard, a light shone around him, and he heard the answer to his questions: The most important person in the world is the one you are with. The most important place is here, where you are now. And the most important thing is to do good for the person you are with, for it was for such that we were placed in this life.

And then the young man was happy.

1 Peter 4:10—"Like good stewards of the manifold grace of God, serve one another with whatever gift each of you has received."

Do you recall the first time you heard a Bible story? Where were you, and who told it to you?

Write a memory story here: _____
_____
_____
_____
_____
_____
_____
_____

CHAPTER FOUR

Singing Silly Songs

♪ *I've got the joy, joy, joy, joy down in my heart.* ♪

Dear Grandmother,

A link is forged when persons laugh together. Laughter jumps across age barriers. Laughter is a wonderful relation-building bridge between grandmother and grandchild. Enjoy silly times with your grandchild.

Age teaches us that looking foolish isn't the worst thing that can happen to us, and relationships built on shared fun are more important than dignity.

In singing silly songs, remember that it is not the well-trained voice that counts with grandchildren, but the fun and caring. Don't hold back. Be part of the action. ❧

J.

Children love silly, nonsense songs. Perhaps you, as a child, sang "Miss Lucy Had a Baby" in which the baby drank up the bathtub water and ate up the soap, or "John Jacob Jingleheimer Schmidt" where the "dah, dah, dah," goes on and on, louder and louder. Or consider the silly words of the old song "Clementine."

Did you ever think that some of the exaggerations in the Bible might be humorous? What about Jesus' words about a camel going through the eye of a needle (Matt. 19:24) or "Blind guides! You strain out a gnat but swallow a camel!" (Matt. 23:24)?

To teach truth in a new way, we'll take these Bible verses and add exaggeration and absurdity. In this chapter, we take traditional fun songs and, by changing the words, make them our own Bible songs.

Music has the wonderful property of staying with us. It runs around and around in our heads long after we have stopped singing.

1. MATTHEW 23:24
(SUNG TO TUNE OF "THE OLD GRAY MARE")

Straining out a gnat and swallowing a camel,
Swallowing a camel,
Swallowing a camel,
Straining out a gnat and swallowing a camel,
Ughh! Choke! Yum! Yum! Yum!

Add movement to the last line. Hold your throat and rub your tummy. Exaggerate expressions.

2. MATTHEW 19:24
(SUNG TO TUNE OF "ON TOP OF OLD SMOKY")

I threaded my needle.
It wouldn't go through.
I was using a camel.
What a silly thing to do.

Exaggerate this song by sliding to the right on the first line and holding the last word *(needle)*. Then s-l-i-d-e to the left on the second line and hold the last word *(through)*. Slide back to the right and hold *camel*. Slide to the left on the last line. Sing it silly. Play it big. Make big, dramatic movements and pauses.

3. MATTHEW 10:30
(TRADITIONAL TUNE, INCLUDED)

Oh, it's one, two, three,
I'm counting all my hairs
On my head,
On my head.
Oh, it's four, five, six,
I'm getting in a fix
Counting all the hairs on my head.
Oh, it's seventy, eighty, ninety,
And the spot is only tiny,
On my head,
On my head.
Now I'm in the millions,
And it looks like there are trillions,
Counting all the hairs,
On my head.

Encourage your grandchildren to make up additional counting verses.

Do you know the words for numbers in different languages? It would be fun to sing the numbers in French, German, Spanish, or Japanese. For our grandchildren the world is getting smaller. There are many other languages. It's fun to learn that different sound patterns have been created to express the same idea.

COUNTING ALL HAIRS

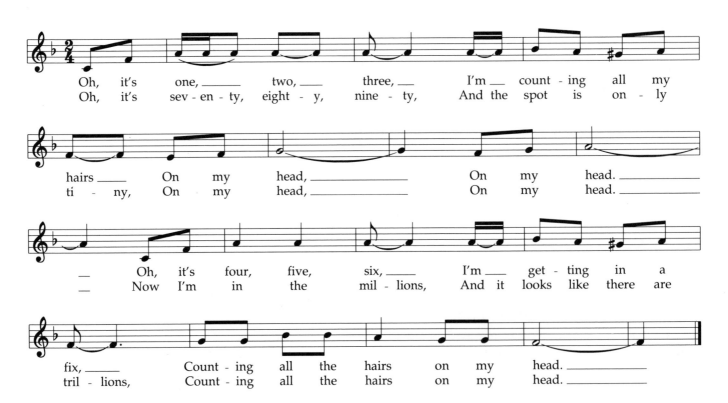

Oh, it's one, _____ two, ___ three, ___ I'm __ count - ing all my
Oh, it's sev - en - ty, eight - y, nine - ty, And the spot is on - ly

hairs ____ On my head, _____ On my head. _____
ti - ny, On my head, _____ On my head. _____

_ Oh, it's four, five, six, ____ I'm __ get - ting in a
_ Now I'm in the mil - lions, And it looks like there are

fix, ____ Count - ing all the hairs on my head. _____
tril - lions, Count - ing all the hairs on my head. _____

4. DEBORAH
(TRADITIONAL NONSENSE SONG, INCLUDED)

We need to affirm our biblical women role models. Deborah, in the Old Testament, is such a model. To help your grandchildren remember Deborah, connect her story with a traditional nonsense song.

Read from a children's Bible or a Bible storybook Judges 4:1-16, or tell the story in your own words.

Emphasize how the Israelite army was much smaller than the army of Sisera. Tell how the Israelites feared the large army, who had iron chariots from which the soldiers threw spears and shot arrows at their enemy. But the Israelites followed their leader, Deborah, and trusted God to help them.

Tell the story of the rain falling and the rivers swelling and the nine hundred chariots sinking into the mud. Then sing:

> Mud, mud, glorious mud.
> Sisera's army was stuck in the mud.

(Say: "Deborah said to Sisera:)

> Follow me, follow,
> Down to the hollow.
> Your chariots will wallow,
> In glorious mud."

MUD, MUD, GLORIOUS MUD

Don't be surprised if your grandchild says, "Let's sing it again."

Encourage your grandchild to use contemporary dance steps to the mud song. It's amazing to me that even very young children seem to be aware of popular dance steps. They can teach you and keep Granny up-to-date.

5. A TRADITIONAL JIGSAW BIBLE SONG

An old favorite children's song is "Bingo." You probably sang it as a child. First, the name is spelled completely, then each time you sing it again you leave out a letter of the name and clap instead.

In this version, we begin by singing and clapping a biblical name, then go on to sing and clap the grandchild's name. Add the names of all her friends.

Jesus had a special friend
And Peter was his name, sir
   P-E-T-E-R
   P-E-T-E-R
   P-E-T-E-R
And Peter was his name, sir.

If your grandchild's name has five letters, like "Laura" or "Megan" or "Brian" or "Danny," substitute that name for "Peter."

For a four-letter name like "Paul" or "Bret" or "Sara" or "Jane," begin with a clap, then spell the name.

Names with more than five letters don't fit the rhythm but can be squeezed into the tune if your are a quick-tongued grandmother. Be prepared for gales of childish laughter.

6. THROW IT OUT THE WINDOW

Review favorite Bible stories and make up your own verses. Almost any Bible story that can be squeezed into the tune will turn out funny when you "throw it out the window." For example:

THROW IT OUT THE WINDOW

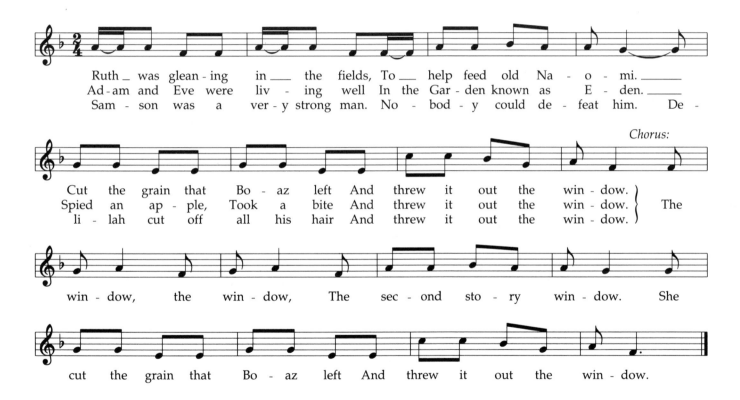

Ruth _ was glean - ing in ___ the fields, To __ help feed old Na - o - mi. _____
Ad - am and Eve were liv - ing well In the Gar - den known as E - den. _____
Sam - son was a ver - y strong man. No - bod - y could de - feat him. De -

Chorus:

Cut the grain that Bo - az left And threw it out the win - dow. ⎫
Spied an ap - ple, Took a bite And threw it out the win - dow. ⎬ The
li - lah cut off all his hair And threw it out the win - dow. ⎭

win - dow, the win - dow, The sec - ond sto - ry win - dow. She

cut the grain that Bo - az left And threw it out the win - dow.

Ruth was gleaning in the fields,
To help feed old Naomi
Cut the grain that Boaz left,
And threw it out the window.

Chorus:

The window, the window,
The second story window.
She cut the grain that Boaz left
And threw it out the window.

Adam and Eve
Were living well
In the Garden known as Eden.
Spied an apple.
Took a bite.
And threw it out the window.
etc.

Samson was a very strong man.
Nobody could defeat him.
Delilah cut off all his hair.
And threw it out the window.
etc.

Daniel in the lion's den.
As brave as he could be.
He looked that lion in the eye.
And threw him out the window.
etc.

And don't forget those silly Bible songs you learned as a child: "Father Abraham" and "Arky, Arky." Recall other childhood favorites.

Funny things your grandchild said or sang:

CHAPTER FIVE

In Grandmother's Attic

♪ *I sing a song of the saints of God, patient and brave and true.* ♪

Dear Grandmother,

An attic, a basement, or a storage room can be a magical place for a grandchild. Let's look at some of the things you might find there.

An old trunk or barrel can be the container for cast-off finery and provide hours of fun and entertainment, playing dress-up. Be alert at garage sales and church white elephant sales for inexpensive items to add to your dress-up trunk. Include scarfs, feathers, fans, and especially hats. Evening dresses are great favorites, as well as shawls, old bathrobes, men's ties, old Halloween costumes, old handbags, and costume jewelry.

If you sew, save those leftover scraps and remnants of material: royal material like velvet and silk and lace, coarse material like burlap and monk's cloth. Even jars of buttons provide fun.

There is something magical about dress-up. Donning a costume frees us, releases inhibitions. We hear Bible stories in a new way. In this section, we dress up for a number of Bible stories. In addition, we use old playing cards to experience a Bible story, and we look at our Christmas decorations as we hear a story.

Explore your own storage area with your grandchild and discover your treasures. ❦

F.

A PEACOCK PARADE

A really well-stocked dress-up trunk would enable you to act out Isaiah 3:18—the finery of the *anklets,* the *headbands,* and the *crescents,* the *pendants,* the *bracelets* and the *scarves,* the *headdresses,* the *armlets,* the *sashes,* the *perfume boxes,* and the *rings,* the *festal robe,* the *mantles,* the *cloaks,* and the *handbags,* the garments of *gauze,* the *linen* garments, the *turbans,* and the *veils.*

Try to find all of these items and pile them on. You may have to find out what some of the words are, or just imagine what they might mean.

When the child is dressed, have a Peacock Parade. Walk like a peacock, displaying the finery. If you have simple rhythm instruments like bells or kazoos or sticks, accompany the parade with music. Make up words to sing or hum.

MAKE A SIGNET RING

Haggai 2:23b—"[I will] make you like a signet ring; for I have chosen you," says the LORD of hosts.

In your accumulation spot, is there a jar of old buttons? If so, you can make a signet ring.

In ancient times, a signet ring was given to special people to show they had power and authority. Your grandchild is special, and God is our king.

Choose a button. Slip a pipe cleaner through the hole in the button. Twist the pipe cleaner to fit around your grandchild's finger. Cut off the ends.

Make up a play about a signet ring.

JOSEPH'S COAT

Cut the form of a coat from a large piece of cardboard; the side of an old box will do. Bring out your material scrap box, glue, and scissors.

Read or tell the Bible story of Joseph's coat of many colors to your grandchildren (Genesis 37).

Give them space and freedom to create Joseph's coat, cutting up scraps of the material and gluing it onto the cardboard, overlapping the edges. It's an interesting effect to put all predominantly blue scraps together; all red ones, and so on. The scraps can combine plaids, solids, stripes, or whatever you have.

If you have lots of chiffon or gauze scarves in a variety of colors in your dress-up trunk, the children can "dance" Joseph's coat. Holding a scarf in each hand, twirl around, making big, sweeping circles in the air with the scarves. Grandmother can join in the dance.

DRESS FOR A FEAST

Many Bible stories tell of or conclude with a great feast. These stories give your grandchildren opportunity to dress to the hilt. For example, a description of a banquet given by King Ahasuerus in Esther 1 says: "The king gave for all the people present in the citadel of Susa, both great and small, a banquet lasting for seven days, in the court of the garden of the king's palace. There were white cotton curtains and blue hangings tied with cords of fine linen and purple to silver rings and marble pillars." Quite a banquet! Drinks were served in golden goblets as the diners reclined on couches of "gold and silver on a mosaic pavement of porphyry, marble, mother-of-pearl, and colored stones." Do you have any old dishes around? Set a banquet table. Use draperies and sheets to create the elegant banquet setting.

After the banquet, King Ahasuerus decided to choose the most beautiful maiden in the land to be his queen. Esther was chosen.

Dress up as Esther.

Then tell the rest of the wonderful story of how Queen Esther saved her people. Esther had a big problem to solve, and she did it!

This whole story is full of dress-up characters: Mordecai in sackcloth and ashes, kings and queens in royal robes. Memorize Esther 4:14b: "Who knows? Perhaps you have come to royal dignity for just such a time as this." Stretch your grandchild's imagination with the question: "I wonder if you were born for a very special time and service. What do you think?"

COVENANT CAPE

When David, the young shepherd boy, killed the giant Goliath and fought bravely against the Philistines, King Saul asked him to live in the royal palace. There he met Jonathan, King Saul's son, and David and Jonathan became best friends. The Bible says, "Jonathan loved him as his own soul" (1 Sam. 18:1). They made a covenant of friendship together; and in token of his covenant, Jonathan gave David his cape.

Create a covenant cape from the dress-up box. Any piece of material approximately 18" X 24" will do. Something like red felt would be elegant. Pin or stitch a piece of ribbon to one end of the material. This ribbon will tie in a bow around the neck.

Even more simple would be to use an old silk bathrobe and tie the sleeves around the child's neck, or use a fancy apron, tying the apron strings around the neck.

Pantomime is an ancient form of communication using only the body, no words. After creating the cape, invite your grandchild to tell the story of Jonathan and David using only body movements and props. What body movements show friendship? What facial expressions? How would you present the cape? You be David to your grandchild's Jonathan. Then reverse roles. It is fun, and pantomime can translate knowledge into expressive action.

Try to capture in your pantomime the generosity, the sharing, the fun of being a friend and what a special blessing you have when your grandchild is also your friend!

RED HAT

Is there a red hat in your dress-up box? If so, this one's for you. I heard about a beautiful Korean custom whereby on reaching age sixty-one, a grandmother was presented with a red hat. This hat symbolized wisdom gained through years of living. Every year thereafter the grandchildren come to their grandmother to review the year and ask her advice and wisdom. What a lovely custom!

OLD PLAYING CARDS

Does your attic contain a box of old games with pieces missing—left over from being loved when your own children were small? And are there lots of playing cards without a full deck in the whole pile? Consider yourself lucky. These are great for creating Nehemiah's wall and a fun way to spend a rainy afternoon with your grandchild.
Recall the story for the children.

Jerusalem had been captured. The walls that once surrounded and protected the great city were torn down, and all the homes destroyed. Most of the people were marched away to be slaves.

Many years passed. A noble, young Jewish man named Nehemiah was a slave who waited on King Artaxerxes. Nehemiah heard about how bad the once beautiful city of Jerusalem looked. It made him so sad he wept. The king noticed his expression and asked what was wrong. Nehemiah explained. Then he said (and this was very bold for a slave), "May I return to Jerusalem and rebuild the wall?" The King not only agreed but sent soldiers to escort him and permitted him to get wood to rebuild the gates of the wall.

When the people living in Jerusalem heard Nehemiah's plan they rejoiced, and all agreed to help. This was how Nehemiah proposed to rebuild the wall: Everyone would repair the portion of the wall in front of his home and others would work on the stretches between.

Now the fun begins. Space the children around the room. Give each grandchild some playing cards to build a wall; first in front of himself, then extending as far as possible to reach the next grandchild.

I tried this with four elementary-age children. The only walls I could build were tepee type structures, and they kept falling. Soon I was amazed at what the children were accomplishing. Each of the four was constructing something a little different. All walls were standing, and some were two and three stories high. Soon the walls met and covered the entire room. The children were so proud. No one wanted to take the walls down.

CHRISTMAS DECORATIONS

Are your Christmas decorations packed away in the attic? As familiar as many of the decorations are from being used year after year, there is always something new and exciting about getting them out again. Special memories are often attached to ornaments. Share these memories with your grandchild. As you get ready for Christmas, or at any time of the year, open the box where you keep your Christmas decorations and share this story with your grandchildren:

Once upon a time there was a little girl who was not happy about her Christmas tree. She had seen a pink, fluffy tree with sparkling plastic decorations in a department store window. When she got home and saw her old-fashioned green Christmas tree she began to pout.

"This old tree is wobbly and decrepit! And look at all these old ornaments. Why can't we have something new and shiny? I wish our tree could have something special about it."

Her mother overheard her grumbling and said: "It has something very special. It has sentiment."

When her mother left, the little girl continued to grumble: "Sentiment. Now, what is that supposed to mean?"

Then, much to the little girl's surprise, the tree began to speak: "Sentiment means associations with the past. It means that this tree and all the things on it are objects that have been associated for a long, long time with the Christmas story and with your family members."

The little girl didn't want the tree to know how impressed she was that it could speak, so she said, "Big deal."

"Now, just a minute," the tree continued. "I am full of secrets and surprises and memories. The ornaments on my branches tell of deeds of great courage and love."

But the little girl continued to mumble: "It looks to me like it is full of sagging ornaments and unmatched decorations and hand-me-down trinkets. I don't mean to hurt your feelings, but why do we have Christmas trees anyway?"

And the tree's voice took on a dreamy quality and it began to intone: "According to a legend that all of us trees believe because our great-grandparents told our grandparents, who told our parents, who told us, the first Christmas tree was revealed by a miracle one Christmas Eve about twelve hundred years ago. Saint Boniface was an English missionary monk. He was trying to bring the story of Christianity to Germany. One Christmas Eve he came upon a group of people who didn't know about God and Jesus, and worshiped a vengeful god, Thor. They thought the way to please their god was to offer him a human sacrifice, and there they were, standing in a solemn circle around this big oak tree, ready to kill the young son of the chieftain. Just as one of the men raised his mighty ax to kill the boy, Saint Boniface rushed up, grabbed the ax, and began to chop down the mighty tree. The people crouched in fear and horror because they thought this tree was sacred and their god would do something terrible to all of them. The tree fell to earth with a mighty, thunderous noise that echoed far into the forest. As it fell, it split into four pieces, and (here's the miracle) from its very center there grew a young evergreen. The people slowly uncovered their eyes, lifted their heads, and looked in amazement. Saint Boniface said, 'This little tree, a young child of the forest, shall be your holy tree. It is the sign of an endless life, for its leaves are always green. It points to heaven. Take this little tree into your home. Instead of surrounding it with deeds of blood, surround it with loving gifts and acts of kindness.'

"And ever since, we have had living green Christmas trees to remind us of the time when the people saw the miracle of that little evergreen and learned that the Christ Child brings peace and promises eternal life. Pink, fluffy trees, indeed!"

"I didn't know that story," the little girl said quietly.

Strange things continued to happen to the little girl as she stood by her Christmas tree. Next the stars on the tree began to speak. *(If you have stars in your decoration box, bring one out now as you continue the story.)*

The stars said: "We have a story, too. According to a story that all of us Christmas tree stars believe, because our great-grandparents told our grandparents, who told our parents, who told us, there was once, and only once, a great blazing star that behaved as no other star before or after ever has behaved. It was brighter and bigger, with a blazing trail of fire, and it moved across the sky when it wanted to, and it could stop and direct its light to a special place when it wanted to. It was the Star of Bethlehem. And it was this special star that caused three very old, very wise men to leave their homes and travel on a long, tiring journey to an unknown destination. They saw the star and said, 'Some very great thing is coming to the world. Whatever it is, the world has never seen anything like it before.' And they followed the star and found the baby Jesus. And now we have stars on our Christmas tree to remind us of the time when the wise men followed a star to Bethlehem."

The stars had been twinkling as they were speaking. Now their light faded, and the shiny balls on the tree began to glow and then speak. *(If you have glass-ball Christmas decorations and other ornaments, bring them out now.)*

"At first," the balls said, "Christmas trees were hung with fruit. Then glass balls in beautiful colors replaced the fruit. Then the decorations began to have different shapes." *(Take out your decorations and share personal stories of where the ornaments came from, who gave them to you, and so on. What is your oldest ornament? Do you have any your grandchild made? Add these stories to the other story. Then continue.)*

On this little girl's magical tree even the tinsel began to speak: "According to a legend that all of us Christmas tree tinsel believe, because our great-grandparents told our grandparents, who told our parents, who told us, there was once a poor woman who was unable to provide any trimmings for her children's Christmas tree. She put the children to bed on Christmas Eve and then sat crying until she fell asleep. Some friendly little spiders heard her and wanted to help. They climbed slowly and carefully back and forth, up and down the tree, spinning their silvery webs until the entire tree was covered. When the children rushed in to see the tree the next morning, all the cobwebs had turned to silver. With the sun shining on them, it was the most beautiful tree in the whole town. And so, now we put tinsel on our trees to remind us of that night."

"I love that story. Thank you," said the little girl.

The tree said, "Even my pine cones have something to say to you."

And sure enough, the very pine cones on the tree began to speak: "According to an ancient legend that all of us cones believe, because our great-grandparents told our grandparents, who told our parents, who told us, we go back to a Christmas Eve long, long ago. There was once a poor mining family living in the forest. The father became ill and unable to work, and the mother and children had no food or fuel. Every morning the mother would go deep into the forest to pick up cones to sell as fuel. But the family was becoming poorer and poorer and more and more ragged and more and more hungry. It was Christmas Eve, and the mother had been unable to buy any gifts or food for the family. This day she went farther into the forest than she had ever gone before. She came upon a tree she had never seen before and quickly filled her basket to overflowing with the cones. As she walked home, her basket became heavier and heavier. Several times she had to stop and rest. She would like to have taken out some of the cones to lighten her load, but she knew how much her family needed them, so she plodded on. When she reached home and emptied her basket, she found, to her amazement, that all the cones had turned to pure silver."

"Now," the tree asked, "are you beginning to understand what I meant when I said this tree was full of secrets and surprises and memories?"

"Oh, yes, yes," the little girl replied.

"And one last thing, the best of all. What is it your mother puts under the tree every year?"

(Bring out your nativity characters. Let your grandchild identify the characters. Read from your Bible Luke 2:1-7.)

"In those days a decree went out from Emperor Augustus that all the world should be registered. . . . All went to their own towns to be registered. Joseph also went from the town of Nazareth in Galilee to Judea, to the city of David called Bethlehem, because he was descended from the house and family of David. He went to be registered with Mary, to whom he was engaged and who was expecting a child. While they were there, the time came for her to deliver her child. And she gave birth to her firstborn son and wrapped him in bands of cloth, and laid him in a manger, because there was no place for them in the inn."

"So here I am," said the tree. "Just an old-fashioned Christmas tree, covered with scores of objects that remind us of former Christmases. A tree that celebrates the birth of Jesus, the Holy Babe of Bethlehem. A tree that ties in ancient legends and stories that people have loved for years. A tree that belongs uniquely to your family. I'm so much more than a decoration for a room. I am a living symbol of family happiness. Now, do you understand what your mother means by *sentiment?*"

The little girl sighed. "Yes, we have the most wonderful Christmas tree in the world."

You and your grandchild draw some of your favorite Christmas Ornaments in this space:

Holding Grandmother's Hand

♪ *All things bright and beautiful, all creatures great and small.* ♪

Dear Grandmother,

   When your grandchild reaches up and takes your hand, you know the trust, the love, the let's-have-an-adventure feeling. Walking hand in hand, you can teach, encourage creativity, discover the world around you, and just have fun.

   One of the most moving sights I have ever seen was the cast, in a museum in Nairobe, Kenya, of what might be the very first human footsteps ever found. What touched me so deeply about these footsteps was that just beside the adult prints were the tiny footprints of a child. Back in some prehistoric dawn, they were walking hand in hand. In this chapter we walk with our grandchild indoors and out, in the city and the country. We hurry, and we wait—hand in hand.

J.

MOVING ALONG

Walking out-of-doors, hand in hand with your grandchild is a special blessing. A child is so curious, active, and lively. You will discover in these walks that there is no such thing as an ordinary experience, only a series of unusual events. Many times we, as adults, melt the event down to the ordinary, but not with a child along.

As you walk along hand in hand with your grandchild, you soon discover he or she does not just walk at a measured pace. Part of the delight of walking with a grandchild is the variety of movements you will experience. Swinging, jumping, running, sliding, swaying, and skipping will be a part of even the shortest walk.

You might look together at the movement you see in nature. Watch birds in flight. Observe how the tops of trees are almost always moving. Let the child imitate these movements. Movement to a child is the most expressive of skills. The staccato pattern of rain might inspire an original rain dance. Bending, shaking, and twisting, the child can imitate the growth of a flower. Encourage grandchildren to move like the animals they see—hopping like a rabbit, jumping like a grasshopper, flitting like a butterfly, squatting like a frog, gliding like an eagle.

WALKING IN THE WOODS

When walking in the woods with your grandchild, don't always stay on the path or trail. Let the beckoning of a bright berry or flower call you. Often the most beautiful wildflowers are hidden. What a delight to look under brush for a Jack-in-the-Pulpit, to come upon Doll's Eyes, to push back the leaves and see the red roots of Bloodroot. Look for flowers with three leaves. There are more than thirty species of the three-leaf trillium wildflower found in Northern woods and bogs and on Southern mountains. Look for shamrocks and clover. Caution! Learn to identify those poisonous three-leaf plants: poison ivy, poison oak, and poison sumac.

Nature has much to teach us. The touch-me-not flowers grow close to poison ivy and nettles, healing their neighbors.

Endless time can be spent looking at trees. Discover strange twistings and burls as a tree adjusted to its environment. Talk about the flexibility and strength of trees. They must stand firm through storms and droughts. Invite your grandchild to choose a favorite tree and tell you why.

Crunch through small obstacles and enjoy the sound. Or walk as silently as you can toward chipmunks or birds. Try to walk as the Native Americans did, stepping first on the outside of one foot, then silently rolling toward the inside of the foot. Follow the same pattern on the other foot. Children love to try this, and it is good for teaching grace and balance.

Make a game of stepping over fallen trees or branches without touching. Discover other outdoor places to duck under or squeeze through without touching. See if you can pass through a nature area and leave it as undisturbed as before you came.

OUR LIVES IN EXPANDING CIRCLES

Find a place for you and your grandchild to sit outdoors with a panoramic view if possible and also something interesting close at hand to look at.

Begin by experiencing personal circles. Make circular motions with hands and feet. The child may turn around in a circle. Circle your head around.

Now extend your awareness beyond your body just a few feet, to nearby grasses, leaves, rocks. Are there any circle patterns in this section? Look intensely and with focus.

After a time, broaden the awareness—twenty to thirty feet away. Feel that everything you see is a part of you. You are in an expanding circle.

Now, extend your awareness to distant ridges—into the vast blue sky.

Feel your place in the vast circle of the universe. Join hands with your grandchild and swing around and around. Those who have lost their roots in the earth miss the very meaning of life.

End this experience by sharing some doughnuts!

ECHOES

In your outdoor walks, can you find an "echo" place? On a mountain or at the mouth of a cave or anyplace that vibrates back the sound will do. A large empty warehouse works in the city. Have fun experimenting with echoes. Clap and listen for the response. Try out different voices: high voices, low voices, silly voices. Share this story:

Two boys met on a mountaintop.

"Hi" said the first boy. "What are you doing?"

"I'm up here talking to this echo, and he is the meanest, rudest echo you've ever heard."

"Really?"

"I'll just show you what I mean," said the second boy, and he cupped his hand to his mouth and shouted, "Shut up!"

"Shut up!" replied the echo

"I hate you!"

"I hate you!" came back the echo.

"Drop dead!"

"Drop dead!" repeated the echo.

The second boy turned to the first one. "See what I mean?"

"Let me try," said the first boy, and he cupped his hands to his mouth and shouted, "Hello there!"

"Hello!" came back the echo.

"Would you like to come play?"

"Come play," replied the echo.

"You sound nice."

"Nice."

The second boy turned to the first boy, and said, "Well, I don't get it. The echo is nice to you, but he sure is rude to me."

Jesus said, "Do unto others as you would have them do to you."

SEASONS RIDDLES

Walking hand in hand out-of-doors makes us very aware of the seasons. All seasons bring their unique joy. To help focus your grandchild's awareness of the nature around her at each season try this game/chant.

While I was walking in the Spring
I happened to see the funniest thing
What was it?

(Child looks all around and supplies an answer. How many answers can you come up with?)

While walking on a Summer day
This thing was standing in my way.
What was it?
(Again, the child supplies answers)
I was walking on a coolish day in the fall
And I saw the strangest thing of all.
What was it?
(Child answers)
Walking one day in the Winter light
I came upon this joyful sight.
What was it?
(Child answers)

RESTING

After these movement experiences of excitement and heightened activity children tire quickly, and so does Grandmother. For a rest, some quiet, and a change of pace, you might try imitating a rock. Sit very still and quietly. Be a rock. This gives you time to recoup on your walk, to gather your energy, to let the strength of the rock flow through you.

Or sit in a beautiful place and choose a happy memory to think about. Teach your grandchild to treasure the quiet moment. Learn this Bible verse: "Be still, and know that I am God!" (Ps. 46:10).

An older grandchild can enjoy sitting quietly outdoors for a long period of time to observe the animal life. Without sudden noise or movements squirrels, birds, and spiders will go about their natural activities.

You may prefer to spend the quiet time looking at the clouds. All sorts of patterns and shapes move before your eyes—animals, funny faces, ships. Make up a story about the cloud characters.

BACKYARD WALKING

A Summer Idea

If you are a gardening grandmother, walk hand in hand with your grandchild around your own backyard or garden. Have a smelling adventure. Move slowly and quietly, stopping often to sniff. Try to determine where scents are coming from. Perhaps you grow fragrant flowers like roses, lilacs, or hyacinths. Maybe you have a herb garden with lemon balm or thyme or sage or mint. Pinch off a few leaves and crush and smell them. A child may lie down sniffing and rolling in fresh cut grass or leaves. Smell leaves on bushes. Discover sweet-smelling vines like honeysuckle. Ask: "What do you think the Garden of Eden smelled like? What smell of spring flowers greeted Jesus on Easter morning? What does heaven smell like?"

Think about smells. What are your very favorite? In Japan it is traditional to go to view cherry blossoms and then to write a poem. Try this with flowers from your garden.

A Winter Idea

Perhaps snow has fallen during the night of your grandchild's visit. Suddenly everything is covered with white. Dress in warm clothes and go out and play a backyard snow-tracking game. You and your grandchild stand side by side in untracked snow. Then turn your backs to each other and walk in a wide circle in opposite directions until you are back where you started. (You'll pass each other on the way.) Now, go around the circle again backward, stepping in each other's tracks. Try not to miss the tracks.

Make "snow angels" by lying in the snow and moving your arms up and down at your sides to create wings. Remind your grandchild of the Christmas angels' "good tidings of great joy."

WALKING IN THE CITY

While walking in the city, look for all the things people have done to make our walking easier. Someone laid the sidewalk. Someone cleaned the street. Someone planned the stoplight and figured out how to coordinate it.

Thank you. Every job well done has dignity.

Draw below a map of a walk, hand in hand with your grandchild.

WHILE WE WAIT

In our modern world a lot of time is spent waiting—waiting in line, waiting in offices, waiting for someone to come, waiting for public transportation. Waiting sometimes causes a child to be cross, impatient, and sleepy. If you are in a situation of waiting with your grandchild, be prepared with some waiting games. Here are some emergency ideas:

Copy Drawing

Have in your purse a pad of paper and colored pencils. Instead of handing them to the child and saying, "Draw something," try copy drawing. Each of you takes one sheet of the paper. The grandchild draws a line on his paper. You copy it exactly on your paper. The grandchild continues the picture, pausing to let you copy exactly, in color, shape, and size. Try as hard as you can to copy the picture exactly. It is not as easy as you might think. This teaches us to look very carefully, and it's fun. Then have a parent guess who drew which picture. Can you fool the parent?

Copy drawing can be an ongoing activity with your out-of-town grandchild. My granddaughter loves to draw. It is her favorite means of self-expression. She came up with the idea of copy drawing and often sends me a picture to copy-draw and return to her. I don't know what it means to Sarah-Neel, but it has an interesting effect on me. As I observe the picture as intensely as I can and try to copy—in texture, shape, and design—I am aware of her uniqueness. I can never get it exactly the same. As I copy flying persons and strangely colored animals, I am allowed to enter her very private fantasy world, and my life is enriched.

Trying to completely empty myself and enter her world is amazing. The challenge is to see without judging. I realize how strong is my desire to have the child be a certain way, derived from my background and my experience of living. This predisposition prevents me from giving the unconditional love that children need. Copy drawing helps me to realize this. Each child is unique—a gift from God—a manifestation of God. Our primary task is to love unconditionally.

I think this would be an interesting experience with a musical child. He or she could tape a melody for you to sing back, antiphonally; or you could share this experience on a musical instrument. The child becomes the teacher, and you are allowed to learn. Our grandchildren have much to teach us.

Magic Rubbing

Are there stray objects in your pocketbook, such as a coin, a button, a paper clip? Place the object under a piece of paper. The child rubs with a crayon, and the object appears. Three-year-old Laura, giving directions for this activity, said, "You just take a crayon. Go back and forth and back and forth, and it just comes."

Heart Drawing

Draw a big heart on your sheet of paper. Tell your grandchild to put into the heart everyone who loves the child and whom he or she loves.

Doodle Waiting

Make patterns on the paper. Many beautiful patterns based on the letter V or on triangular and acute angle shapes can while away the time. For example:

1. Draw a line of V's connecting. The child colors the upper section in one color, the lower section in another color. Then the child draws another line of pattern V's directly under the first line of patterns. The child colors this in. Continue with the pattern to fill the page.

2. The same idea can be used with numbers. Draw three large 3's in a line. The child repeats with another line of 3's underneath, equally spacing the figures. Continue until the page is filled. Now fill in with colors. If the number 3 is repeated in one line and the paper is turned around until the 3's are upside down and then another line of 3's is drawn above it, then the paper is inverted and another line of 3's is drawn under the last line; this continued will form another pattern. This idea was told to me by a grandmother in Kenya. Typical African line patterns found on pottery, gourds, wooden vessels, and combs are created in this manner.

Doodle Patterns

Here is a doodle waiting idea: Draw two inch squares all over a sheet of paper. Instruct the child to fill the squares with patterns, using only *straight* lines. How many can you come up with? This is especially good for elementary age and older children.

Doodle a Snowflake

Perhaps you are waiting on a snowy day. Looking at a snowflake, we are looking at one of nature's most profound mysteries. How can beauty and structure arise from such a delicate balance? A man named Bentley photographed 5,000 snowflakes and found that no two were alike. All were six-sided, but all were different.

Doodle as many six-sided snowflakes as you can. Make them all different.

In addition to drawing, there are waiting games and stories.

Look for Things

From wherever you are sitting, look all around. Go through the alphabet, looking for things. What do you see that starts with an A? B? And so on through the alphabet.

Look for colors. Taking turns, each of you names something that is a certain color. For example, "I see a brown chair." "I see a green plant." The color cannot be repeated.

Waiting Story

Imagine that the grandchildren are at your house. It is time for a parent to pick them up. Everything has been gathered together, and the children are sitting, waiting, ready to go. Begin an imaginary story:

"Your mother is on her way. She is walking out of the office."
"No!"
"She forgot her book, she has to go back." *(pause)*
"Now she is coming."
"No!"
"The telephone rings, and she has to run back and answer it." *(pause)*
"Now she is coming."
"No!"
"Her shoe came untied, and she has to sit down and tie it or she may fall." *(pause)*
"Now she is coming."
"No!"
"She can't find the car keys. She is rummaging through her purse." *(pause)*
"Oh, she finds them. Now here she comes."

"No!"

"She has to stop and pick up some milk." *(pause)*

The story goes on and on with all the little interruptions that *could* happen on the way. Stop at any time you see the mother actually coming and say, "And here she is." Sometimes the children get into the story and add imaginary things that could be happening. If the parents are very late, your imagination will get a good workout.

Play Stand-a-Minute

You will need a watch with a second hand for this game. Tell the grandchild of elementary age to begin standing for exactly one minute when you say "Go." When she thinks a minute has passed, she sits down. This is harder than it sounds. Sometimes the child sits in as short as twenty seconds. Sometimes she stands for a minute and a half. Don't tell the exact time until she sits. Usually the child will say, "Let's do it again," and it will probably be different.

Car Seat Songs

It gets very tiring on long car rides for little children strapped in a car seat. This is a great time for singing. Try "Hokey Pokey." This gives the young child a chance to stretch: "You put your right hand in, and shake it all about," etc. Holding the hands high in the air, swaying to the left and right, bouncing up and down to rhythm provides relaxation and fun.

In the close confines of a car, try singing rounds like "Row, Row, Row Your Boat" or "Sweetly Sings the Donkey." Front seat and back seat, sounds vibrating, bouncing around the walls, will keep the child entertained.

Without being able to run and stretch, make a game of discovering everything you can wiggle-wobble—fingers, hands, arms, head, shoulders, legs, feet, tongue, ears, elbows, and so on.

SAYING GRACE IN A PUBLIC RESTAURANT

Because of noise or other conditions it is sometimes difficult to say a blessing in a restaurant setting.

At the time of Jesus' ministry the Jews had a ritual of Berakah, which was a blessing of bread at the beginning of a regular family meal.

Picking up on this idea, take the bread or crackers that are usually served before a meal at a restaurant. Pass it around to the members of the family, instructing each to break off a piece. Holding a piece of the bread in their hands, the family looks at each other as Grandmother, Grandfather, or another member of the family says, "We break this bread in thankfulness to God for our abundance and in remembrance of Jesus."

Then all eat together. This ritual can even be observed at a fast food restaurant. The point is that all share a common piece of bread and pause together to remember and thank God.

If grandchildren live out of town, you can still hold hands in prayer.

Children delight in knowing that you and they are praying at the same time. If you have many grandchildren, set a specific time for each to pray. There is strength and comfort in each other's praying presence.

A SPECIAL "GOOD-BYE"

A terrible letdown descends on most grandparents when their grandchildren leave after a noisy, hectic visit. Phyllis Theroux captured this feeling: "You're almost too close to the meaning of life with small children. It takes your breath away." So leave them with a smile.

When it is time to say good-bye to your grandchild, a special expression used repeatedly leaves you with warm feelings. Children love rhyming words.

"See you later, alligator."

"After while, crocodile."

Make up your own, or better, let your grandchild create one. Discover how much fun you can have with words.

"So long, Ping-Pong."

"Take care, teddy bear."

"Be cool."

"Adios."

These good-byes are affirmations of love, of continuity, of hope, of wishing your dear ones well.

Good-bye. God be with you.

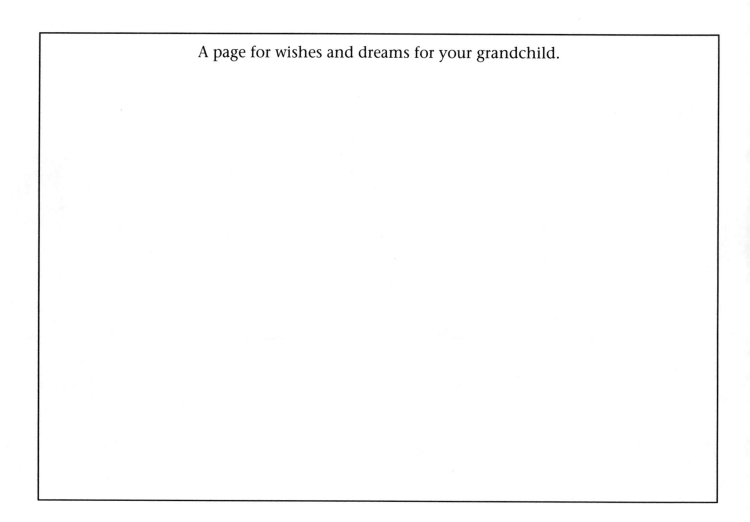

A page for wishes and dreams for your grandchild.

A page for wishes and dreams for your grandchild.

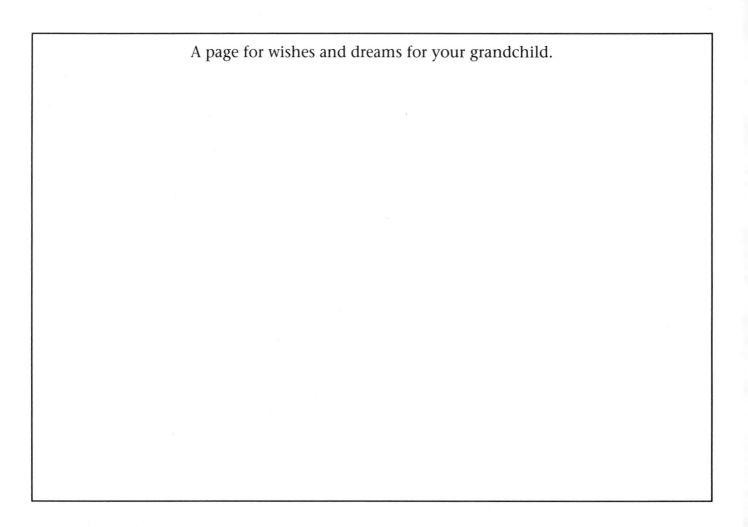

A page for wishes and dreams for your grandchild.

A page for wishes and dreams for your grandchild.

A page for wishes and dreams for your grandchild.

A page for wishes and dreams for your grandchild.

Judy Gattis Smith

With Granddaughters
Sarah-Neel Smith and Laura Rush Scott